THE

SHOWDOWN

It's Going Down

Keisha G Knight

The Showdown

Table of Contents

CHAPTER I

FINAL CONFLICT

September 2023 - 21 Days Fasting and Prayer. September 1st to September 21st, 2023.

I am beginning to document my experience on the third day of my 21-day fast.

September 3rd 2023
As soon as I decided to write, the title "Showdown, It's Going Down" popped into my head. I didn't have to think about it or consider any other words. The title presented itself clearly and succinctly: "The Showdown, it's going down."

I must say that God is wiser than my thoughts. Last month, in August 2023, I felt disconnected from the current spiritual events, even though the Holy Spirit was guiding me. However, everything I saw and heard still pointed to the Tribulation and the soon return of Jesus. I felt as though there was still a disconnect in my understanding of spiritual events, which God allowed. I felt that the only way for me to truly comprehend what God was revealing to me was through fasting and praying. I yearned to connect with Him and surrender myself to another 21-day fast.

The Showdown

I believe that God instilled in me the desire to connect with Him and surrender to fasting and praying. God is wise. This is how He reveals deep things to me, and through this, I can see more clearly. He allows His Holy Spirit to show me supernatural visions. Sometimes, fasting for just one day is not enough to understand spiritual events. The current distractions - both global and domestic - are creating a fog, and those who won't listen or see remain in this fog. Who won't hear, will not hear and who cannot see, will not see. However, I trust in God's mercy and guidance. ***Jesus is coming soon!***

(Jeremiah 5:21 KJV) "Hear this now, O foolish people, Without [a]understanding, Who have eyes and see not, And who have ears and hear not:"

It seems that there are many concerning events happening around the world, from the Pope's Laudato si meetings and discussions around climate change, to politicians and politics, the ongoing COVID-19 pandemic, natural disasters like earthquakes, volcanoes, and mudslides, widespread wildfires, conflicts like the Ukraine-Russia war, and issues like lawlessness, drug trafficking, and false prophets. Additionally, there are rumors of wars, bloodshed, and discussions around the implementation of digital dollars, as well as the potential construction of a third temple. Despite all of this, it appears that many people in the USA are not particularly concerned, especially when it comes to the future of the cash dollar. This lack of concern is somewhat strange.

According to Matthew 24:7, nations and kingdoms will rise against each other, leading to famines, diseases, and earthquakes in various places.

(Matthew 24:12 KJV) "And because iniquity shall abound, the love of many shall wax cold."

The Showdown

Many people seem to be more interested in the latest dance moves, celebrity events, and AI (artificial intelligence), regardless of whether it goes against their religious beliefs or not. The rapid growth of AI and mankind's increasing knowledge is also a topic of interest. Additionally, there is more news coming out of institutions like CERN, regarding talks about other universes. However, it seems that people have become increasingly self-centered and hateful towards each other. We have reached our tipping point and are now facing; **The Final Conflict!**

(2 Timothy 3:2-4 KJV)
"2 For men shall be lovers of their own selves, covetous, boasters, proud, blasphemers, disobedient to parents, unthankful, unholy,
3. Without natural affection, trucebreakers, false accusers, incontinent, fierce, despisers of those that are good;
4. Traitors, heady, highminded, lovers of pleasures more than lovers of God;"

Note: I asked "AI - artificial intelligence" software on my friend's computer, in July 2023.
Is AI (artificial intelligence) an increase in man's knowledge?
Answer: Yes.

We already knew that this is all part of the Tribulation; that is what our Father God has told me.

(Daniel 12: 4 KJV) "But thou, O Daniel, shut up the words, and seal the book, even to the time of the end: many shall run to and fro, and knowledge shall be increased."

I am not saying that God will definitely reveal something more to me during this fast beyond what He has already revealed; The Tribulation Has Begun. If nothing more is revealed, just being close to Him, staying in the secret place, is more than I can ask for. God is sweet, and we magnify His name. We are born to worship Him. I love the Lord.

(John 15:7 KJV) "If ye Abide in me, and my words abide in you, ye shall ask what ye will, and it shall be done unto you."

On this 3rd day of September 2023, I felt a push from the Holy Spirit to start documenting my experiences. Although I did not feel compelled to do so during the recent 21 days of fasting for the year 2023, I trust that God knows best and has a reason for prompting me now. While I have previously taken notes during my times of fasting and prayer, when God moves you, nothing can stop it. Amen.

From Day 1 until today, which is Day 3 (9/1/2023 - 9/3/2023)
It has been quiet. It feels like I am just resting with God.
During my previous periods of fasting and prayer, I have observed that it is around Day 7 and beyond that I begin to feel and see things with greater spiritual clarity. At this time, God seems to strip away my distractions, straighten me out, and prepare my heart for a deeper connection with Him. It is only when I start to experience the uncomfortable withdrawal symptoms of denying myself what I want when I want it, that I am truly able to delve into the depths of my faith. Despite the humbling nature of this experience, it is a beautiful and intimate time of walking closely with God.

I also usually feel a bit sick and sniffly (under the weather) during the first few days. I prayed to God to please be easy on me in this regard.

Today, Aunt Mavis had another health episode. She was sitting in her wheelchair and suddenly passed out. Just like before, God to the rescue. He got me to her in time and provided the necessary nursing care. I helped her to bed, elevated her legs, prayed for her, and made sure she was comfortable. Thankfully, she recovered quickly.

Aunt Mavis is now 96 years old, and it is an honor and privilege to be able to care for her. Every day with her is a blessing, and I am grateful for the opportunity to give her the best possible care every day as long as God allows it.

(Psalms 23: 6 KJV) "Surely goodness and mercy shall follow me all the days of my life: and I will dwell in the house of the Lord forever."

As I close this night's notes, I must say that I give thanks for life, truly.

(1 Thessalonians 5:18 KJV) "In everything give thanks: for this is the will of God in Christ Jesus concerning you."

And that's why as long as I live and have breath, I will praise the Lord!!

(Psalms 146:2 KJV) "While I live will I praise the Lord: I will sing praises unto my God while I have any being."

Day 4 - 9/4/2023

Today, as I am pondering on the message that God is communicating to me regarding this fast'; The Showdown, It's Going Down. I feel prompted to reflect, revisit, and record the past 21 days of fasting and prayer leading up to this fast, September 2023. Additionally, it seems like God is asking me to document my previous fasts and prayers in reverse order, starting from the most recent one to the earliest.

The Showdown

Now, let's revisit the prior 21 Days of Fasting and Prayers: Going Backwards.

CHAPTER II

THY WILL BE DONE

May 2023 - 21 Days of Fasting & Prayer
Thy will be Done

(Isaiah 4 KJV) "And in that day seven women shall take hold of one man, saying, We will eat our own bread, and wear our own apparel: only let us be called by thy name, to take away our reproach.

2. In that day shall the branch of the LORD be beautiful and glorious, and the fruit of the earth shall be excellent and comely for them that are escaped of Israel.

3. And it shall come to pass, that he that is left in Zion, and he that remaineth in Jerusalem, shall be called holy, even every one that is written among the living in Jerusalem:

4. When the Lord shall have washed away the filth of the daughters of Zion, and shall have purged the blood of

Jerusalem from the midst thereof by the spirit of judgment, and by the spirit of burning.

5.   And the LORD will create upon every dwelling place of mount Zion, and upon her assemblies, a cloud and smoke by day, and the shining of a flaming fire by night: for upon all the glory shall be a defence.

6.   And there shall be a tabernacle for a shadow in the day time from the heat, and for a place of refuge, and for a covert from storm and from rain."

"We will eat our own bread". Mercy.

But those who are in Christ can always seek refuge in the Lord by keeping His promises, trusting & obeying Him, even when others don't choose to follow him.

(2 Timothy 3: 2 KJV) "For men shall be lovers of their own selves, covetous, boasters, proud, blasphemers, disobedient to parents, unthankful, unholy,"

During my fast in May 2023, I received a clear message from God that can be summed up as "Thy Will Be Done". This message was different from previous ones that I had received during my 21-day fast and prayers. It wasn't just a warning or a sign of things to come, but a final verdict. God declared that his will would be done, and there were no more signs to look out for. It is time to prepare for his coming without any hesitation.

(Luke 21:28 KJV) "And when these things begin to come to pass, then look up, and lift up your heads; for your redemption draweth nigh."

The Showdown

It seems the Lord is simply saying: It's Over! The Final Plan, I AM ON MY WAY!
This is great news for a sinner saved by grace, like me. The wages of sin is death, I choose to live.

(Romans 6:23 KJV) "For the wages of sin is death; but the gift of God is eternal life through Jesus Christ our Lord."

People's minds are being pulled to and fro.

(Matthew 6:24 KJV) "No man can serve two masters: for either he will hate the one, and love the other; or else he will hold to the one, and despise the other. Ye cannot serve God and mammon."

(1 Kings 18:21 KJV) "And Elijah came unto all the people, and said, How long halt ye between two opinions? if the Lord be God, follow him: but if Baal, then follow him."

CHAPTER III

BACK TO EGYPT

1/2023 - 21 Days Fast & Prayer
        Back to Egypt

The greatest gift God blessed me with is to fast and pray. One of my biggest revelations is that there is a place. A place I can go where I am close to God. A secret place, a safe place, a real place that is shielded by God's grace.

(Psalms 91:1 KJV) "He that dwelleth in the secret place of the most High shall abide under the shadow of the almighty."

This should be one's daily endeavor. To stay close to God always and to stay connected to the vine.

(John 15:5 KJV) "I am the vine, ye are the branches: He that abideth in me, and I in him, the same bringeth forth much fruit: for without me ye can do nothing."

This fast was quite intriguing. I can say that I was shocked. I didn't really see this information coming, but, it came.

The Showdown

(Deuteronomy 12:32 KJV) "What things soever I command you, observe to do it: thou shalt not add thereto, nor diminish from it."

A ton of information, taking us way back, "BACK TO EGYPT". My eyebrows were now in a shocked position. What is it, God? He said, the very place that I delivered you from, is the very place that the devil is trying to pull you back to. For centuries, long decades of the devil and his constant schemes of trying to pull us back to idol/sun worship - Back To Egypt.

(Exodus 9:1 KJV) "Then the LORD said unto Moses, Go in unto Pharaoh, and tell him, Thus saith the LORD God of the Hebrews, Let my people go, that they may serve me."

(John 8:36 KJV) "If the Son therefore shall make you free, ye

shall be free indeed."

It is us - we, you, and I that keep going back into bondage. It happens and we don't even realize it. The devil has remained relevant throughout history. He uses all his tricks and plays, mixed with the current events of the day, to pull us right back to slavery. His game is deception, he wants to trick and play with our minds. The devil wants to be worshiped.

(Luke 22:31-32 KJV) "And the Lord said, Simon, Simon, behold, Satan hath desired to have you, that he may sift you as wheat:
But I have prayed for thee, that thy faith fail not, and when thou art converted, strengthen thy brethren."

The devil's pervasive influence is ubiquitous. It is in the things we see, use daily, and are prescribed to. There are idols all around us,

14

around our children, in our families, homes, schools, churches, etc. The world has been permeated with lies by the devil. Now, I know why there is nothing new under the sun and that the devil is the father of lies.

(John 8:44 KJV) "Ye are of your father the devil, and the lusts of your father ye will do. He was a murderer from the beginning, and abode not in the truth, because there is no truth in him. When he speaketh a lie, he speaketh of his own: for he is a liar, and the father of it."

(Ecclesiastes 1:9 KJV) "The thing that hath been, it is that which shall be; and that which is done is that which shall be done: and there is no new thing under the sun."

The devil will try and try to deceive us with his lies. He wants to con us out of our heavenly kingdom. He wants to play with our minds to entice us to follow and worship him.

(Jeremiah 13:23 KJV) "Can the Ethiopian change his skin, or the leopard his spots? then may ye also do good, that are accustomed to do evil."

Here are some words that flowed through my mind during this fast: Kraken, Euphrates, idol worship, cop convention (image of their logo - represents the sun/sun worship), the sun god (Ra), sun god worship, etc.
With each word that flowed, I would ask God as to what is the connection to Egypt is. He then would send me on a research, all guided by his Holy Spirit. After seeing the connection, I am in tears. All I can say is, my my my. We have been terribly tricked. All those years to escape Egypt, to now recognize that we have been inching our way back. God Help us!

The Showdown

I see a correlation between sun god worship and the papacy. At the "cop" convention(s), You can see their business logo displayed. A business or brand logo represents and defines what one stands for. Their logo represents the sun and worship of the sun, which are All the systems of the devil. Dietes/ra/baal etc.
Note: The same logo is displayed at CERN, on movies, dances, celebrities, political figures, and many more.

We do not bow or worship the sun. We do not worship two masters. We worship God, our Lord and Savior, Jesus Christ. He said that if we love Him, we are to keep his commandments, then he will speak to the Father, and then we will receive the Holy Spirit that will lead us and guide us into all truth.

(John 14:15-16 KJV) "If ye love me, keep my commandments.
And I will pray the Father, and he shall give you another Comforter, that he may abide with you for ever;"
I clearly understand why God says to Remember, Remember the Sabbath Day! He tells us that He is the Lord, thy God, our Creator. We ought to obey and keep his commandments and to love Him with all our might and soul.

(Matthew 22:37 KJV) "Jesus said unto him, Thou shalt love the Lord thy God with all thy heart, and with all thy soul, and with all thy mind."

(Exodus 31:13 KJV) "Speak thou also unto the children of Israel, saying, Verily my sabbaths ye shall keep: for it is a sign between me and you throughout your generations; that ye may know that I am the LORD that doth sanctify you."

(Exodus 20: 8 - 11 KJV)

"Remember the sabbath day, to keep it holy Six days shalt thou labour, and do all thy work But the seventh day is the sabbath of the Lord thy God: in it thou shalt not do any work, thou, nor thy son, nor thy daughter, thy manservant, nor thy maidservant, nor thy cattle, nor thy stranger that is within thy gates:
For in six days the Lord made heaven and earth, the sea, and all that in them is, and rested the seventh day: wherefore the Lord blessed the sabbath day, and hallowed it."

The Sabbath would be the biggest deception the devil will use against God's people.

(Daniel 11:31 KJV) "And arms shall stand on his part, and they shall pollute the sanctuary of strength, and shall take away the daily sacrifice, and they shall place the abomination that maketh desolate."

There is only one individual who stands guilty of attempting to sit on God's throne. Driven by his desire for worship, he was cast down from heaven to earth. He seeks to replicate all that God has created, and he impersonates God to deceive His children.

(Revelation 12: 7-9 KJV) "And there was war in heaven:
Michael and his angels fought against the dragon; and the dragon fought and his angels,

> And prevailed not; neither was their place found any more in heaven.
> And the great dragon was cast out, that old serpent, called the Devil, and Satan, which deceiveth the whole world: he was cast out into the earth, and his angels were cast out with him."

The Showdown

The Lord's holy day has never changed. From the Old Testament to the New Testament, the Sabbath, the seventh day, Saturday, has never changed.

I just had an exciting thought regarding how God reveals information to me. It reminds me of the sequences of events in the books of Revelation and Daniel from the Bible. Sometimes, it seems like events unfold in reverse order, or that the full understanding of them comes later. That's why I'm excited; because I understand that I must wait, listen, trust, obey, and keep walking in faith.

(Hebrews 11:6 KJV) "But without faith it is impossible to please him; for he that cometh to God must believe that he is, and that he is a rewarder of them that diligently seek him."

(Psalm 37:34 KJV) "Wait on the LORD, and keep his way, and he shall exalt thee to inherit the land: when the wicked are cut off, thou shalt see it."

CHAPTER IV

PROMISE KEEPER

Day 5 - (9/5/2023)

I woke up this morning with the desire to have a conversation with you about some of my personal experiences and how I dealt with them. You know, those situations where I had to trust and believe in the Lord and truly stand on his word to make it through. The times when I had to cling to His promises even when I couldn't see, think, or imagine. FAITH!

(Ephesians 3:20 KJV) " Now unto him that is able to do exceeding abundantly above all that we ask or think, according to the power that worketh in us,"

I hope that my personal journey can inspire you to strengthen your spiritual life. Faith is a daily pursuit and we must be aware of the constant attacks from the enemy, who aims to produce guilt and doubt within us. It's important to know that the devil will never stop trying to weaken our belief in Jesus, but we must remain steadfast and never give up. Don't stop believing!

(2 Chronicles 15: 7 KJV) "Be ye strong therefore, and let not your hands be weak: for your work shall be rewarded."

(James 4:7 KJV) "Submit yourselves therefore to God. Resist the devil, and he will flee from you."

I am honored to still be caring for my aunt Mavis, who is now 96 years old. I have been given to her as an assignment from God. I have now been her caretaker for over 5 years. She is still in the land of the living and we praise God daily for his blessing on her life. She is bedridden now and yes, it is a lot more of a responsibility to care for her, but God always seems to give me the strength to care for her. I will persist with the grace of God. God continues to be my daily and unwavering source of assistance.

(Psalm 28:7 KJV) "The Lord is my strength and my shield; my heart trusted in him, and I am helped: therefore my heart greatly rejoiceth; and with my song will I praise him."

STRAIGHT IS NOT STRAIT

(Matthew 7: 13-14 KJV) "Enter ye in at the strait gate: for wide is the gate, and broad is the way, that leadeth to destruction, and many there be which go in thereat:
        Because **strait** is the gate, and narrow is the way, which leadeth unto life, and few there be that find it."

        When I spiritually matured, I realized that the pathway to righteousness is not broad or just a "perfect size 2". No, not at all. The path can become a bit ruff, restrictive, lonely, bumpy, and corrective but it will lead you on the right pathway to life everlasting.

The path that God has called us to follow is not easy.

(Hebrews 12: 2 KJV) "Looking unto Jesus the author and finisher of our faith; who for the joy that was set before him endured the cross, despising the shame, and is set down at the right hand of the throne of God."

Over the past few weeks, I have noticed that not only myself but other saints as well are feeling weary and tempted. We are being distracted and losing focus from the cross. It seems that the prayer line, which was initiated during the COVID-19 pandemic as a gathering place for Kingdom families, is now losing its members. The attendance rate is going down. Even I am feeling distracted and sometimes unable to keep up with my daily prayer line responsibilities. Initially, I was bothered by this, but then I remembered that the Lord constantly reminds me that He is able to keep me from falling.

I WILL KEEP YOU FROM FALLING

(Jude 24-25 KJV) "Now unto him that is able to keep you from falling, and to present you faultless before the presence of his glory with exceeding joy,
To the only wise God our Saviour, be glory and majesty, dominion and power, both now and ever. Amen."
God reminded me that it is he that keeps us and not we ourselves. He is the one who ascended, that his very spirit - the Holy Spirit, can descend on us to teach us and guide us in all ways. He has blessed us with many spiritual gifts. All of us have a role to play in this heavenly kingdom, and whatever God has started in your life, He will complete it. My job is to seek the kingdom first! God will handle the rest.

(Psalms 100: 3 KJV) "Know that the Lord he is God: it is he that hath made us, and not we ourselves; we are his people, and the sheep of his pasture."

(John 16:13 KJV) "Howbeit when he, the Spirit of truth, is come, he will guide you into all truth: for he shall not speak of himself; but whatsoever he shall hear, that shall he speak: and he will shew you things to come."

(Ephesians 4: 11-12 KJV) "And he gave some, apostles; and some, prophets; and some, evangelists; and some, pastors and teachers; For the perfecting of the saints, for the work of the ministry, for the edifying of the body of Christ:"

God will do anything to save his children. He Loves us.

(2 Chronicles 7:14 KJV) "If my people, which are called by my name, shall humble themselves, and pray, and seek my face, and turn from their wicked ways; then will I hear from heaven, and forgive their sin, and will heal their land."

This is why I am no longer bothered when his sheep, which are called by his name, stray away. He shows me that he is my Shepherd.

(Psalm 23:1 KJV) "The Lord is my Shepherd; I shall not want."

KEEP MY EYES FIXED ON CHRIST

I must remain loyal to God. If I call out to him and keep my eyes on the cross, I will not sink. He pointed me to Peter.

(Matthew 14: 22-31 KJV) And straightway Jesus constrained his disciples to get into a ship, and to go before him unto the other side, while he sent the multitudes away.

23. And when he had sent the multitudes away, he went up into a mountain apart to pray: and when the evening was come, he was there alone.
24. But the ship was now in the midst of the sea, tossed with waves: for the wind was contrary.
25. And in the fourth watch of the night Jesus went unto them, walking on the sea.
26. And when the disciples saw him walking on the sea, they were troubled, saying, It is a spirit; and they cried out for fear.
27. But straightway Jesus spake unto them, saying, Be of good cheer; it is I; be not afraid.
28. And Peter answered him and said, Lord, if it be thou, bid me come unto thee on the water.
29. And he said, Come. And when Peter was come down out of the ship, he walked on the water, to go to Jesus.
30. But when he saw the wind boisterous, he was afraid; and beginning to sink, he cried, saying, Lord, save me.
31. And immediately Jesus stretched forth his hand, and caught him, and said unto him, O thou of little faith, wherefore didst thou doubt?

When you are a child of God, you can call out to him and he will save us! He is always willing and able to save us.

(Isaiah 65:24 KJV) "And it shall come to pass, that before they call, I will answer; and while they are yet speaking, I will hear.

(2 Peter 3:9 KJV) "The Lord is not slack concerning his promise, as some men count slackness; but is longsuffering to us-ward, not willing that any should perish, but that all should come to repentance."

What a mighty God we serve. He makes things happen in due season.

(Galatians 6:9 KJV) "And let us not be weary in well doing: for in due season we shall reap, if we faint not."

September 5th thru the 12th 2023, the fasting and prayer are progressing smoothly. When I say well, I'm speaking about the cravings for things. I am learning that the more I spend time fasting and praying, those cravings disappear. My days are mostly filled with listening to sermons, articles and having conversations about God. I enjoy opportunities to practice love and spend more quality time with the Lord. Many days I must remind myself to eat after the day's fast has ended. I am truly enjoying surrendering to fasting and praying. It gives you strength, willpower, and a Godly dependency to depend on God alone.

September 13th - As I stated in the beginning, there are some fasts and prayers, through which God just keeps me close. He tells me about myself and reasons with me on matters of the heart. Of course, I always think and wait in great expectation for a new or brighter revelation of things and of things to come regarding the end times that we are currently living in and His soon return. I would say that I am a bit inquisitive about knowing the real deal about what's going on in this world, but one cannot rely on the media or any other source except the Word Of God, for information. Amen.

"OTHER BOOKS OF THE BIBLE". As this day's fast and prayer was almost at its close, those were the words that came into my thoughts.

There were times, as an adult, when I read a few books outside the books of the
Bible (the 66 Books) that were originally introduced to me as a child. By the way, I was baptized and raised as a child in the Seventh Day of Adventist religion, I am a sabbath keeper.

I was now curious to know what God was trying to reveal. I was pushed to look for others in the Bible whose names are mentioned, but they did not write a book. (Per my initial 66 Books of the Bible's understanding).

I found a few names, but I was led directly to Gad the Seer. Who was Gad the Seer?

Gad is a prophet associated with King David. His name is mentioned just a few times in the Bible. After doing some reading about Gad, one main moral or point that kept sticking out to me, is that he was bold, respected, and unapologetic in doing and saying what he was told. He was not afraid to speak about unpleasant things.

This is the text that rested in my heart as I pondered this BOLDNESS.

(Hebrews 4:16 KJV) "Let us therefore come boldly unto the throne of grace, that we may obtain mercy, and find grace to help in the time of need."

Daily, I ask God for the boldness to go forth. I do strive daily to work on my belief in him and what he says about me. I admit that it is me that keeps getting in my own way. I am so thankful though, he constantly reminds me that all I need is a grain. A grain of mustard seed. He is more than able and capable of filling all my voids, needs, and lacks. He will lead me, direct me, purge me, and clean me with hyssop; he will keep me. All he wants me and all of us to do is to allow him.

The Showdown

(Matthew 17:20 KJV) "And Jesus said unto them, Because of your unbelief: for verily I say unto you, if ye have faith as a grain of mustard seed, ye shall say unto this mountain, Remove hence to yonder place; and it shall remove; and nothing shall be impossible unto you."

(Psalm 51:7 KJV) "Purge me with hyssop, and I shall be clean: wash me, and I shall be whiter than snow."

September 16th, 2023 Sabbath Brooklyn Public Library (Music Entertainment rapper - Jayz mural)

Day number 16 of these 21 days of fasting and prayer is here and it's the Sabbath day. Daily, I seek to understand the information that God has been revealing through this fast and put it all together. However, I am still awaiting direct revelation through this fast. I am honored to always sit with the Lord. He has been strengthening my faith. When he says that:

(Isaiah 41:10 KJV) "Fear thou not; for I am with thee: be not dismayed; for I am thy God: I will strengthen thee; yea, I will help thee; yes, I will uphold thee with the right hand of my righteousness."

Believe It!

It is me that must align with what God says about me daily.
Believing that what God says; He Will Do It!
What he feels about me and promises me, I MUST believe him.

(John 14:12 KJV) "Verily, verily, I say unto you, He that believeth on me, the works that I do shall he do also; and greater works than these shall he do; because I go unto my Father."

The Showdown

(Hebrews 11: 6 KJV) "But without faith it is impossible to please him: for he that cometh to God must believe that he is, and that he is a rewarder of them that diligently seek him."

Sabbath worship today was a blessing as usual. I attended my home church in the Park Slope area in Brooklyn, New York City. While driving on my way home, God instructed me to stop the car. Get out of the car, he said, and head over to the Brooklyn public library. The Brooklyn Public Library is located by the Grand Army Plaza. Currently, there is a feature on the building by a famous entertainment rapper named Jayz. It is some sort of exhibit that features his musical work. I was not quite sure as to why or what I was looking for, but I will go.

(Psalms 25:5 KJV) "Lead me in thy truth, and teach me: for thou art the God of my salvation; on thee do I wait all the day."

Now I have been to this library many times as a child growing up. That was because the high school I attended as a youth was close by. As a member of the track team, it was at the library that I and my fellow teammates would make our daily stop. It was there that we would change from our school clothing into our exercise gear before track and field practice. The park in which we practice daily is just across the street, Prospect Park. Of course, there were many other times in which I utilized the library for homework and to do research.

This visit to the library was a bit different. It felt as though I was on a spiritual assignment and that my eyes must be opened to look for and see things from a spiritual lens, even though the main assignment was not clear as yet. I am, however, very present with the knowledge that the devil wants to take us back to Egypt. Knowing that, made me very enthused to go, so I grabbed my phone to take pictures.

The Showdown

On approaching the building, I first noted the structure that is used for this exhibit. The building resembles an ancient, yet modern, palace, temple, or coliseum. Then I saw the rapper's musical words display that covered the entire front view of the building. The format of words and paragraphs looked like the formatting seen in the Bible. The lyrics are from the rapper's album; The Book of Hov. He refers to himself as Jehovah. I did not spend much time focusing on the words as I was more drawn to the entrance of the building. The building's entrance has what resembles two pillars on either side. On these pillars, with one on the right and one on the left, there are images that I have noted from various Egyptian depictions. At this point, I am still not sure that I saw what I really came to see. But then, as soon as my eyes finished scouring the two pillars, with my head tilted all the way up, I saw it.

There were three images of the sun right above my head in the doorway's entrance, each with a light bulb in the middle. Then I glimpsed into the far right corner of the right pillar and saw an image of a man. A man bowed on his knees before another image of a sun, as if worshiping the sun. I left the library shortly after.

Brooklyn Public Library

The Showdown

(Exodus 20: 3-5 KJV) "Thou shalt have no other gods before me.
Thou shalt not make unto thee any graven
image, or any likeness of
anything that is in heaven above, or that is in the earth beneath, or
that is in the water under the earth.
Thou shalt not bow down thyself to them, nor serve them: for I the
Lord
thy God am a jealous God, visiting the iniquity of the fathers upon
the third and fourth generation of them that hate me;"

I came home and pondered all the information from today and revisited all the information going back to the first day of this 21-day fast and prayer. I am still not clear as to what God is showing me concerning the world; however, I do know and I do feel his strength strengthening me daily, leading me. I feel his amazing, almighty power, working in my life.

(Philippians 4:13 KJV) "I can do all things through Christ which strengtheneth me."

Days 18 - 21 In these final days of this fasting & praying, God spent time reasoning with me. He instructed me to meditate daily on his word. The more time that I spend with God and in his word, the more I feel closer to him. My personal walk and relationship with him grows, the more that I submit myself to his will. I am strengthened and I can walk boldly in Faith knowing that God's grace is sufficient. It is a daily walk in which God also promises daily new mercies if we just ask.

(Matthew 7:7 KJV) "Ask, and it shall be given you; seek, and ye shall find; knock, and it shall be opened unto you:"

The Showdown

(Joshua 1:8 KJV) "This book of the law shall not depart out of my mouth; but thou shalt meditate therein day and night, that thou mayest observe to do all that is written therein; for then thou shalt make thy way prosperous, and then thou shalt have good success."

I trust him and believe in every word he says that he will fulfill his plans for our lives. He wants me to cling to him and also be reassured that he is with me, guiding me and that he will never leave me.
I know that God is a Promise Keeper. He keeps his word with us. He is more than willing and totally able to save us. God's covenant is an eternal bond.

(Deuteronomy 7:9 KJV) "Know therefore that the Lord thy God, he is God, the faithful God, which keepeth covenant and mercy with them that love him and keep his commandments to a thousand generations;"

(Numbers 23:19 KJV) "God is not a man, that he should lie; neither the son of man, that he should repent: hath he said, and shall he not do it? or hath he spoken, and shall he not make it good?"

My daily duty is to seek the kingdom first and let God handle the rest. Amen

(Matthew 6:33 KJV) "But seek ye first the kingdom of God, and his righteousness; and all these things shall be added unto you."

God has plans for us and he will deliver us from the snares of the devil. Whatever the good Lord has set for you to do, do it. He will provide for you and sustain you. Do not be afraid, because you are not alone. Stand and be of good courage, for our God is with us.

(Jeremiah 29:11 KJV) "For I know the thoughts that I think toward you, saith the Lord, thoughts of peace, and not of evil, to give you an expected end."

(Joshua 1:9 KJV) "Have not I commanded thee? Be strong and of a good courage; be not afraid, neither be thou dismayed: for the Lord thy God is with thee whithersoever thou goest."

God is a Promise Keeper!

(Philippians 1:6 KJV) "Being confident of this very thing, that he which hath begun a good work in you will perform it until the day of Jesus Christ:"

CHAPTER V

ISRAEL

(Genesis 3:15) "And I will put enmity between thee and the woman, and between thy seed and her seed; it shall bruise thy head, and thou shalt bruise his heel."

Although my 21 days of fasting and praying have ended for September 2023, I still felt as though there was more to this revelation. Maybe I should have fasted longer, I thought to myself. I have never fasted and prayed beyond 21 days as yet, but I do look forward to it in the future. For now, I will keep my eyes, ears, mind humble, and spirit connected to God. I feel that there is more he wants to reveal and last month's fast and prayer were just the beginning of the unfolding.

10/4/2023 Today, the USA did a nationwide security system check. An alert signal was sent to everyone's device with network service. We were told that this event was to take place to check the nation's alert disaster notification system.

10/8/2023 (Sabbath) - World News Events of the Day

The Showdown

Today is my personal one (1) day, of monthly fasting and Prayer and I decided to stay home with Aunty Mavis. Yes, I have dedicated a personal day monthly in which I choose to fast and pray. It is a great idea when you are just starting or attempting to fast and pray. God knows your heart and he will provide the strength. Dedicate a specific day, your personal day, to spend extra time in sweet surrender with the Lord.

Instead of attending church this Sabbath, I decided to watch the church service online. As I arose on this beautiful Sabbath morning, I woke to some terrible world news events and catastrophes that had occurred in the world while I was on my night's rest.

There was an earthquake today in Afghanistan, as well as, an attack on Israel by Gaza. Hundreds lost their lives while attending a music concert festival and others were also kidnapped in Israel. There were many other world events that day and every day, it seems, but it was the attack on Israel that became the main news highlight. So many deaths and so much pain. Mercy.

As I rested this Sabbath in fasting and praying, I fell into a deep place with God. With all the information from the world news events of this morning and events from my prior 21 days fast and prayers, I was pondering. I was in deep thought with the Lord. I now intensely feel that there is definitely more to the revelation and understanding from last month's fast and prayer. But until I get this revelation, and if it comes, I will continue to look up!

(Luke 21:28) "And when these things begin to come to pass, then look up, and lift your heads; for your redemption draweth nigh."

By mid-afternoon, things started to happen. I began to feel the nudge to connect the spiritual dots. My heart and my mind were directed by the Holy Spirit to go back to my notes and pictures that were taken last month. I must revisit the experience I had at the Brooklyn Public Library.

As I looked back at the pictures from the Brooklyn Public Library with the famous rapper's music exhibit; The Book Of Hov, the word "Temple" came to my mind. I said, Father, what is the connection between the end times? The Tribulation, wars, rumors of wars, catastrophes, climate change, the image displayed at the library (the temple), and the attack on Israel?

This is where and how I was guided by the Holy Spirit. It was by using my spiritual lens that I was able to see clearly. It is by listening, obeying, and by waiting on the Lord, that I can understand. In this chapter, I will document the revelation from the journey as it unfolded. It is God himself pointing me to and showing me his word. This is how I received my current insights.

Temple? I thought to myself. I am always hearing talks of a third temple being built in Israel. What is the correlation or the similarity between the "temple-like" structure at the Brooklyn Public Library and the Israelis 'third temple?

Second Temple   Brooklyn Public Library
(2)

THIRD TEMPLE

I saw a vision of two nations fighting for Jerusalem. Jerusalem, a city that is currently home to both Muslims and mostly Jewish Israelis. Jerusalem is a special holy worshiping place for both nations. On the Temple Mount lie structures including the Dome of the Rock, to the north and the Al-Aqsa mosque to the south. In the southwest stands the Western Wall - a remnant of the Second Temple and the holiest site in Judaism.
(3)

The Jewish Israelis are preparing to build their third temple in Jerusalem. The carrying out of this event will lead to an uproar among nations. Nations will fight against nations. **A peace treaty will then be signed by the man of sin, the *man of perdition* himself. It is he that stands up and is revealed in the Third temple, he is the *antichrist*.**

(Psalm 127 KJV) "Except the LORD build the house, they labour in vain that build it: except the LORD keep the city, the watchman waketh but in vain."

(2 Thessalonians 2: 4 KJV) "The man who opposeth and exalteth himself above all that is called God, shewing himself that he is God."

A one-world government will be set in place leading to a time of persecution for those that keep the testimonies of God and the faith of Jesus. Prepare!

(Matthew 24:21 KJV) "For then shall be great tribulation, such as was not since the beginning of the world to this time, no, nor ever shall be."

Persecution is coming to those who keep the commandments of God and the faith of Jesus. Prepare your minds and hearts and God will guide us through. When we see these signs, we know our Lord and Savior, Jesus Christ, is near.

(Revelation 12:17 KJV) "And the dragon was wroth with the woman, and went to make war with the remnant of her seed, which keep commandments of God, and have the testimony of Jesus Christ."

(Luke 21:28 KJV) "And when these things begin to come to pass, then look up, and lift up your heads; for your redemption draweth nigh."

Unless the Lord builds the house they labor in vain.

Who Am I?

Remember: Ishmael & Isaac? - Esau & Jacob?

ISHMAEL
Firstborn son to Father Abraham and his mother Hagar; handmade to Sarah: Abraham's wife. Ishmael and his mother were sent to live in the wilderness. Ishmael, also blessed with nations by God, later grew up and married an Egyptian woman.

ISAAC
2ndborn son to father Abraham and firstborn son with his wife Sarah. Isaac, the father of twins Esau and Jacob. God blessed Isaac with the Promised Nation in which the King, Savior of the World would come.

The Promise which was later handed down to his son, <u>JACOB.</u> *God's redemption plan to save mankind!*

ESAU & JACOB

Jacob (Israel) The Chosen shall bruise Esau's heel.

Jacob would compete with and eventually successfully obtain Esau's birthright from him.

(Genesis 25: 23-26 KJV) "And the LORD said unto her, Two nations are in thy womb, and two manner of people shall be separated from thy bowels; and the one people shall be stronger than the other people; and the elder shall serve the younger.
24 And when her days to be delivered were fulfilled, behold, there were twins in her womb.
25And the first came out red, all over like an hairy garment; and they called his name Esau.
26And after that came his brother out, and his hand took hold on Esau's heel; and his name was called Jacob: and Isaac was threescore years old when she bare them."

Who is currently living in the land of Israel?
Mostly Esau's children (descendants), Edomites (Edom), Israelis.

Esau - The uncalled man of the world - man of the field, cunning hunter.

(Genesis 25:27 KJV) "And the boys grew: and Esau was a cunning hunter, a man of the field; and Jacob was a plain man, dwelling in tents."

WHY WAS GOD UPSET AT ESAU?

What is Esdras 6:9?

Why don't I know a book named Esdras?

2 Esdras 6: 9 " For Esau is the end of the world, and Jacob is the beginning of it that followeth."

Why was God upset at Esau? Why did Esau lose his blessing?
   1.Esau sold his birthright.

   2.Esau married Ishmael's daughter
Mahalath Both nations are Relatives thru marriage.

(Genesis 28:9 KJV) "Then went Esau unto Ishmael, and took unto the wives which he had Mahalath the daughter of Ishmael Abraham's son, the sister of Nebajoth, to be his wife."

Ishmaelites: Arab, Muslim nations are **Married/In-laws/Relatives thru marriage** to Edomites, Esau's descendants called Israelis. (Esau married Mahalath) - These related nations are fighting over Jerusalem.

(Genesis 36 KJV) **"**Now these are the generations of **Esau, who is Edom.**

   2. Esau took his wives of the daughters of Canaan; Adah the daughter of Elon the Hittite, and Aholibamah the daughter of Anah the daughter of Zibeon the Hivite;

3. And Bashemath Ishmael's daughter, sister of Nebajoth.
4. And Adah bare to Esau Eliphaz; and Bashemath bare Reuel;
5. And Aholibamah bare Jeush, and Jaalam, and Korah: these are the sons of Esau, which were born unto him in the land of Canaan.
6. And Esau took his wives, and his sons, and his daughters, and all the persons of his house, and his cattle, and all his beasts, and all his substance, which he had got in the land of Canaan; and went into the country from the face of his brother Jacob.
7. For their riches were more than that they might dwell together; and the land wherein they were strangers could not bear them because of their cattle.
8. Thus dwelt **Esau in mount Seir: Esau is Edom.**
9. And these are the generations of **Esau the father of the Edomites in mount Seir:**
10. These are the names of Esau's sons; Eliphaz the son of Adah the wife of Esau, Reuel the son of Bashemath the wife of Esau.
11. And the sons of Eliphaz were Teman, Omar, Zepho, and Gatam, and Kenaz.
12. And Timna was concubine to Eliphaz Esau's son; and she bare to Eliphaz Amalek: these were the sons of Adah Esau's wife.
13. And these are the sons of Reuel; Nahath, and Zerah, Shammah, and Mizzah: these were the sons of Bashemath Esau's wife.
14. And these were the sons of Aholibamah, the daughter of Anah the daughter of Zibeon, Esau's wife: and she bare to Esau Jeush, and Jaalam, and Korah.

15. These were dukes of the sons of Esau: the sons of Eliphaz the firstborn son of Esau; duke Teman, duke Omar, duke Zepho, duke Kenaz,

16. Duke Korah, duke Gatam, and duke Amalek: these are the dukes that came of Eliphaz in the land of Edom; these were the sons of Adah.

17. And these are the sons of Reuel Esau's son; duke Nahath, duke Zerah, duke Shammah, duke Mizzah: these are the dukes that came of Reuel in the land of Edom; these are the sons of Bashemath Esau's wife.

18. And these are the sons of Aholibamah Esau's wife; duke Jeush, duke Jaalam, duke Korah: these were the dukes that came of Aholibamah the daughter of Anah, Esau's wife

19. These are the sons of **Esau, who is Edom,** and these are their dukes.

20. These are the sons of Seir the Horite, who inhabited the land; Lotan, and Shobal, and Zibeon, and Anah,

21. And Dishon, and Ezer, and Dishan: these are the dukes of the Horites, the children of Seir in the land of Edom.

22. And the children of Lotan were Hori and Hemam; and Lotan's sister was Timna.

23. And the children of Shobal were these; Alvan, and Manahath, and Ebal, Shepho, and Onam.

24. And these are the children of Zibeon; both Ajah, and Anah: this was that Anah that found the mules in the wilderness, as he fed the asses of Zibeon his father.

25. And the children of Anah were these; Dishon, and Aholibamah the daughter of Anah.

26. And these are the children of Dishon; Hemdan, and Eshban, and Ithran, and Cheran.

27. The children of Ezer are these; Bilhan, and Zaavan, and Akan.

28. The children of Dishan are these; Uz, and Aran.

29. These are the dukes that came of the Horites; duke Lotan, duke Shobal, duke Zibeon, duke Anah,

30. Duke Dishon, duke Ezer, duke Dishan: these are the dukes that came of Hori, among their dukes in the land of Seir.

31. And these are the kings that reigned in the land of Edom, before there reigned any king over the children of Israel.

32. And Bela the son of Beor reigned in Edom: and the name of his city was Dinhabah.

33. And Bela died, and Jobab the son of Zerah of Bozrah reigned in his stead.

34. And Jobab died, and Husham of the land of Temani reigned in his stead.

35. And Husham died, and Hadad the son of Bedad, who smote Midian in the field of Moab, reigned in his stead: and the name of his city was Avith.

36. And Hadad died, and Samlah of Masrekah reigned in his stead.

37. And Samlah died, and Saul of Rehoboth by the river reigned in his stead.

38. And Saul died, and Baalhanan the son of Achbor reigned in his stead.

39. And Baalhanan the son of Achbor died, and Hadar reigned in his stead: and the name of his city was Pau; and his wife's name was Mehetabel, the daughter of Matred, the daughter of Mezahab.

40. And these are the names of the dukes that came of Esau, according to their families, after their places, by their names; duke Timnah, duke Alvah, duke Jetheth,
41. Duke Aholibamah, duke Elah, duke Pinon,
42. Duke Kenaz, duke Teman, duke Mibzar,
43. Duke Magdiel, duke Iram: these be the dukes of Edom, according to their habitations in the land of their possession: he is Esau the father of the Edomites."

THE GOD OF ABRAHAM, ISAAC, JACOB

(Exodus 3:15) "And God said moreover unto Moses, Thus shalt thou say unto the children of Israel, the Lord God of your fathers, the God of Abraham, the God of Isaac, and the God of Jacob, hath sent me unto you: this is my name for ever, and this is my memorial unto all generations."

God reaffirms the same covenant with Abraham's son, Isaac:

(Genesis 21: 12 KJV) "And God said unto Abraham, Let it not be grievous in thy sight because of the lad, and because of thy bondwoman; in all that Sarah hath said unto thee, hearken unto her voice; for in Isaac shall thy seed be called."

(Genesis 26:3-4 KJV) "Sojourn in this land, and I will bewith thee, and will bless thee, and unto thy seed, I will give all these countries, and I will perform the oath which I sware unto Abraham thy father;

And I will make thy seed to multiply as the stars of heaven, and will give unto thy seed all these countries; and in thy seed shall all the nations of the earth be blessed."

and later with Isaac's son, Jacob:

(Genesis 28: 1) "And Isaac called Jacob, and blessed him, and charged him, and said unto him, Thou shalt not take a wife of the daughters of Canaan."

(Genesis 28: 14-15 KJV) "And thy seed shall be as the dust of the earth, and thou shalt spread abroad to the west, and to the east, and to the north, and to the south: and in thee and in thy seed shall all the families of the earth be blessed.

And, behold, I am with thee, and will keep thee in all places whither thou goest, and will bring thee again into this land; for I will not leave thee, until I have done that which I have spoken to thee of."

God's redemption plan to save mankind!

GOD'S WORD - JACOB'S NAME, CHANGED TO ISRAEL, By God.

(Genesis 35: 10-11 KJV) "And God said unto him, Thy name is Jacob: thy name shall not be called any more Jacob, but Israel shall be thy name: and he called his name Israel.

And God said unto him, I am God Almighty: be fruitful and multiply; a nation and a company of nations shall be of thee, and kings shall come out of thy loins;"

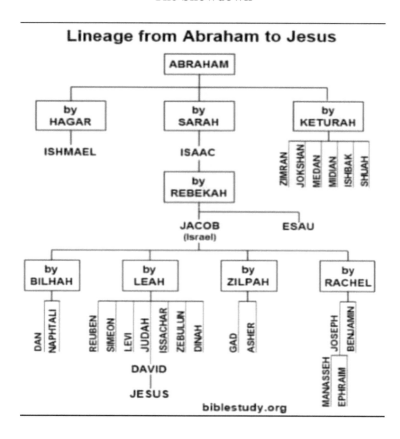

Lineage from Abraham to Jesus

biblestudy.org

(4)

THE CHOSEN PEOPLE

Isaac's 2nd son Jacob (whom God changed His Name to ISRAEL), **is/(are) The Chosen People of God.**

The Messiah, King Jesus Came!!! Through Jacob's (Israel's) lineage, a gift that will be for whosoever, that believes in him. He shall come to be the Saviour to the entire world.

Twins in 1 womb. Esau (1st) & Jacob (2nd). Are they related? Answer: Yes

JACOB (ISRAEL)'S CHILDREN ARE CALLED ISRAELITES

12 TRIBES The twelve sons form the basis for the **twelve tribes of Jacob (ISRAEL),** listed in order from oldest to youngest: **Reuben, Simeon, Levi,** *Judah*, **Dan, Naphtali, Gad, Asher, Issachar, Zebulun, Joseph, and Benjamin.**

THE PROMISED LAND

This land promised to Abraham in Genesis is a picture of covenant faithfulness as God's people pursue their divine calling.
(5)

CANAAN

(Genesis 12:7 KJV) "And the Lord appeared unto Abram, and said, Unto thy seed will I give this land: and there builded he an altar unto the Lord, who appeared unto him."

Canaan is Israel

Canaan is the ancient name of a vast and prosperous country, roughly located in the same place as modern-day Palestine and Israel. This land's heritage is one of abundance, that flows with milk and honey.

(Numbers 14) - THE PEOPLE REJECT CANAAN

Unbelief caused them to view God's promise (the promised land) as evil.

Remember: Noah's son Ham, his descendants of Canaan was cursed. The Canaanites.

Canaanite practices. Leviticus and Deuteronomy contain lurid lists including the worship of demonic idols, taboo sexual acts, and even the sacrifice of children to the Canaanite gods.

(Deuteronomy 9:5) "Not for thy righteousness, or for the uprightness of thine heart, dost thou go to possess their land: but for the wickedness of these nations the LORD thy God doth drive them out before thee, and that he may perform the word which the LORD sware unto thy fathers, Abraham, Isaac, and Jacob."

What is Israel's problem?
 Answer: Disobedience
   REPENT JUDAH, REPENT ISRAEL

(Ezekiel 20:13 KJV) "But the house of Israel rebelled against me in the wilderness: they walked not in my statutes, and they despised my judgements, which if a man do, he shall even live in them; and my sabbaths they greatly polluted: then I said, I would pour out my fury upon them in the wilderness, to consume them."

(Romans 10:21 KJV) "But to Israel he saith, All day I have stretched forth my hands unto a disobedient and gainsaying people."

(Jeremiah 11 1-17 KJV) "The word that came to Jeremiah from the LORD saying,

1.   Hear ye the words of this covenant, and speak unto the men of Judah, and to the inhabitants of Jerusalem;
2.   And say thou unto them, Thus saith the LORD God of Israel; Cursed be the man that obeyeth not the words of this covenant,
3.   Which I commanded your fathers in the day that I brought them forth out of the land of Egypt, from the iron furnace, saying, Obey my voice, and do them, according to all which I

command you: so shall ye be my people, and I will be your God:

4. That I may perform the oath which I have sworn unto your fathers, to give them a land flowing with milk and honey, as it is this day. Then answered I, and said, So be it, O Lord

5. Then the Lord said unto me, Proclaim all these words in the cities of Judah, and in the streets of Jerusalem, saying, Hear ye the words of this covenant, and do them.

6. For I earnestly protested unto your fathers in the day that I brought them up out of the land of Egypt, even unto this day, rising early and protesting, saying, Obey my voice.

8. Yet they obeyed not, nor inclined their ear, but walked every one in the imagination of their evil heart: therefore I will bring upon them all the words of this covenant, which I commanded them to do: but they did them not.

9. And the Lord said unto me, A conspiracy is found among the men of Judah, and among the inhabitants of Jerusalem.

10. They are turned back to the iniquities of their forefathers, which refused to hear my words; and they went after other gods to serve them: the house of Israel and the house of Judah have broken my covenant which I made with their fathers.

11. Therefore thus saith the Lord, Behold, I will bring evil upon them, which they shall not be able to escape; and though they shall cry unto me, I will not hearken unto them.

12. Then shall the cities of Judah and inhabitants of Jerusalem go, and cry unto the gods unto whom they offer incense: but they shall not save them at all in the time of their trouble.

13. For according to the number of thy cities were thy gods, O Judah; and according to the number of the streets of

Jerusalem have ye set up altars to that shameful thing, even altars to burn incense unto Baal.

14.   Therefore pray not thou for this people, neither lift up a cry or prayer for them: for I will not hear them in the time that they cry unto me for their trouble.

15.   What hath my beloved to do in mine house, seeing she hath wrought lewdness with many, and the holy flesh is passed from thee? when thou doest evil, then thou rejoicest.

16.   The LORD called thy name, A green olive tree, fair, and of goodly fruit: with the noise of a great tumult he hath kindled fire upon it, and the branches of it are broken.

17.   For the LORD of hosts, that planted thee, hath pronounced evil against thee, for the evil of the house of Israel and of the house of Judah, which they have done against themselves to provoke me to anger in offering incense unto Baal."

??? Why don't Jacob's children (Israel) know who or identify with who they are?

(John 14: 15-16 KJV) "If ye love me, keep my commandments. And I will pray the Father, and he shall give you another Comforter, that he may abide with you for ever;"

(Hosea 4:6 KJV) "My people are destroyed for lack of knowledge: because thou hast rejected knowledge, I will also reject thee, that thou shalt be no priest to me: seeing thou hast forgotten the law of thy God, I will also forget thy children."

10 COMMANDMENTS

(EXODUS 20 1-17 KJV) "And God spoke all these words, saying,

2.   I am the Lord thy God, which have brought thee out of the land of Egypt, out of the house of bondage.

3.   Thou shalt have no other gods before me.

4.   Thou shalt not make unto thee any graven image, or any likeness of any thing that is in heaven above, or that is in the earth beneath, or that is in the water under the earth.

5.   Thou shalt not bow down thyself to them, nor serve them: for I the Lord thy God am a jealous God, visiting the iniquity of the fathers upon the children unto the third and fourth generation of them that hate me;

6.   And shewing mercy unto thousands of them that love me, and keep my commandments.

7.   Thou shalt not take the name of the Lord thy God in vain; for the Lord will not hold him guiltless that taketh his name in vain.

8.   Remember the sabbath day, to keep it holy.

9.   Six days shalt thou labour, and do all thy work:

10.   But the seventh day is the sabbath of the Lord thy God: in it thou shalt not do any work, thou, nor thy son, nor thy daughter, thy manservant, nor thy maidservant, nor thy cattle, nor thy stranger that is within thy gates:

11.   For in six days the Lord made heaven and earth, the sea, and all that in them is, and rested the seventh day: wherefore the Lord blessed the sabbath day, and hallowed it.

12. Honour thy father and thy mother: that thy days may be long upon the land which the Lord thy God giveth thee.
13. Thou shalt not kill.
14. Thou shalt not commit adultery.
15. Thou shalt not steal.
16. Thou shalt not bear false witness against thy neighbour.
17. Thou shalt not covet thy neighbour's house, thou shalt not covet thy neighbour's wife, nor his manservant, nor his maidservant, nor his ox, nor his ass, nor any thing that is thy neighbour's."

2 GREATEST COMMANDMENTS

(Matthew 22:36-40 KJV) " Master, which is the great commandment in the law?

[37] Jesus said unto him, Thou shalt love the Lord thy God with all thy heart, and with all thy soul, and with all thy mind.
[38] This is the first and great commandment.
[39] And the second is like unto it, Thou shalt love thy neighbour as thyself.
[40] On these two commandments hang all the law and the prophets."

Jacob (ISRAEL)'s Inheritance:

(Ezekiel 48 KJV)

"Now these are the names of the tribes. From the north end to the coast of the way of Hethlon, as one goeth to Hamath, Hazarenan, the border of Damascus northward, to the coast of Hamath; for these are his sides east and west; a portion for Dan.

2. And by the border of Dan, from the east side unto the west side, a portion for Asher.

3. And by the border of Asher, from the east side even unto the west side, a portion for Naphtali.

4. And by the border of Naphtali, from the east side unto the west side, a portion for Manasseh.

5. And by the border of Manasseh, from the east side unto the west side, a portion for Ephraim.

6. And by the border of Ephraim, from the east side even unto the west side, a portion for Reuben.

7. And by the border of Reuben, from the east side unto the west side, a portion for Judah.

8. And by the border of Judah, from the east side unto the west side, shall be the offering which ye shall offer of five and twenty thousand reeds in breadth, and in length as one of the other parts, from the east side unto the west side: and the sanctuary shall be in the midst of it.

9. The oblation that ye shall offer unto the LORD shall be of five and twenty thousand in length, and of ten thousand in breadth.

10. And for them, even for the priests, shall be this holy oblation; toward the north five and twenty thousand in length, and toward the west ten thousand in breadth,

and toward the east ten thousand in breadth, and toward the south five and twenty thousand in length: and the sanctuary of the LORD shall be in the midst thereof.

11.   It shall be for the priests that are sanctified of the sons of Zadok; which have kept my charge, which went not astray when the children of Israel went astray, as the Levites went astray.

12.   And this oblation of the land that is offered shall be unto them a thing most holy by the border of the Levites.

13.   And over against the border of the priests the Levites shall have five and twenty thousand in length, and ten thousand in breadth: all the length shall be five and twenty thousand, and the breadth ten thousand.

14.   And they shall not sell of it, neither exchange, nor alienate the first fruits of the land: for it is holy unto the LORD.

15.   And the five thousand, that are left in the breadth over against the five and twenty thousand, shall be a profane place for the city, for dwelling, and for suburbs: and the city shall be in the midst thereof.

16.   And these shall be the measures thereof; the north side four thousand and five hundred, and the south side four thousand and five hundred, and on the east side four thousand and five hundred, and the west side four thousand and five hundred. [17] And the suburbs of the city shall be toward the north two hundred and fifty, and toward the south two hundred and fifty, and toward the east two hundred and fifty, and toward the west two hundred and fifty.

17. And the suburbs of the city shall be toward the north two hundred and fifty, and toward the south two hundred and fifty, and toward the east two hundred and fifty, and toward the west two hundred and fifty.

18. And the residue in length over against the oblation of the holy portion shall be ten   thousand eastward, and ten thousand westward: and it shall be over against the oblation of the holy portion; and the increase thereof shall be for food unto them that serve the city.

19. And they that serve the city shall serve it out of all the tribes of Israel.

20. All the oblation shall be five and twenty thousand by five and twenty thousand: ye   shall offer the holy oblation foursquare, with the possession of the city.

21. And the residue shall be for the prince, on the one side and on the other of the holy oblation, and of the possession of the city, over against the five and twenty thousand of the oblation toward the east border, and westward over against the five and twenty thousand toward the west border, over against the portions for the prince: and it shall be the holy oblation; and the sanctuary of the house shall be in the midst thereof.

22. Moreover from the possession of the Levites, and from the possession of the city, being in the midst of that which is the prince's, between the border of Judah and the border of Benjamin, shall be for the prince.

23. As for the rest of the tribes, from the east side unto the west side, Benjamin shall have a portion.

24. And by the border of Benjamin, from the east side unto the west side, Simeon shall have a portion.

25. And by the border of Simeon, from the east side unto the west side, Issachar a portion.

26. And by the border of Issachar, from the east side unto the west side, Zebulun a portion.

27. And by the border of Zebulun, from the east side unto the west side, Gad a portion.

28. And by the border of Gad, at the south side southward, the border shall be even from Tamar unto the waters of strife in Kadesh, and to the river toward the great sea.

29. This is the land which ye shall divide by lot unto the tribes of Israel for inheritance, and these are their portions, saith the Lord GOD.

30. And these are the goings out of the city on the north side, four thousand and five hundred measures.

31. And the gates of the city shall be after the names of the tribes of Israel: three gates northward; one gate of Reuben, one gate of Judah, one gate of Levi.

32. And at the east side four thousand and five hundred: and three gates; and one gate of Joseph, one gate of Benjamin, one gate of Dan.

33. And at the south side four thousand and five hundred measures: and three gates; one gate of Simeon, one gate of Issachar, one gate of Zebulun.

34. At the west side four thousand and five hundred, with their three gates; one gate of Gad, one gate of Asher, one gate of Naphtali.

35. It was round about eighteen thousand measures: and the name of the city from that day shall be, The LORD is there."

ISRAEL & JUDAH SCATTERED

(Isaiah 49:6 KJV) "And he said, It is a light thing that thou shouldest be my servants to raise up the tribes of Jacob, ad to restore the preserved of Israel: I will also give thee for a light to the Gentiles, that thou mayest be my salvation unto the end of the earth."

(Jeremiah 29:13 KJV) "And ye shall seek me, and find me, when ye shall search for me with all your heart."

The scattering of Israel & Judah - Assyrians carried the ten northern tribes away into captivity.

(Deuteronomy 4: 27 KJV) "And the LORD shall scatter you among the nations, and ye shall be left few in number among the heathen, whither the LORD shall lead you."

(2 Kings 15:29 KJV) "In the days of Pekah king of Israel came Tiglathpileser king of Assyria, and took Ijon, and Abelbethmaachah, and Janoah, and Kedesh, and Hazor, and Gilead, and Galilee, all the land of Naphtali, and carried them captive to Assyria."

(2 Kings 17:6 KJV) "In the ninth year of Hoshea the king of Assyria took Samaria, and carried Israel away into Assyria, and placed them in Halah and in Habor by the river of Gozan, and in the cities of the Medes."

The scattering continued when Nebuchadnezzar, king of Babylon, carried Judah away into captivity.

(2 Kings 25: 1 KJV) "And it came to pass in the ninth year of his reign, in the tenth month, in the tenth day of the month, that Nebuchadnezzar king of Babylon came, he, and all his host, against

Jerusalem, and pitched against it; and they built forts against it round about."

(2 Kings 25: 7 KJV) "And they slew the sons of Zedekiah before his eyes, and put out the eyes of Zedekiah, and bound him with fetters of brass, and carried him to Babylon."

(2 Kings 25:11 KJV) "Now the rest of the people that were left in the city, and the fugitives that fell away to the king of Babylon, with the remnant of the multitude, did Nebuzaradan the captain of the guard carry away."

THE HORNS THAT SCATTERED JUDAH

(Zechariah 1:18-21 KJV) "Then lifted I up mine eyes, and saw, and behold four horns.

19. And I said unto the angel that talked with me, What be these? And he answered me, These are the horns which have scattered Judah, Israel, and Jerusalem.
20. And the LORD shewed me four carpenters.
21. Then said I, What come these to do? And he spake, saying, These are the horns which have scattered Judah, so that no man did lift up his head: but these are come to fray them, to cast out the horns of the Gentiles, which lifted up their horn over the land of Judah to scatter it."

REVENGE FOR ISRAEL

God will take revenge on the Edomites because they GRIEVOUSLY offended JUDAH.

OFFENSE:

(Obadiah 1 11-14 KJV) "In the day that thou stoodest on the other side, in the day that the strangers carried away captive his forces, and foreigners entered into his gates, and cast lots upon Jerusalem, even thou wast as one of them.

12. But thou shouldest not have looked on the day of thy brother in the day that he became a stranger; neither shouldest thou have rejoiced over the children of Judah in the day of their destruction; neither shouldest thou have spoken proudly in the day of distress.

13. Thou shouldest not have entered into the gate of my people in the day of their calamity; yea, thou shouldest not have looked on their affliction in the day of their calamity, nor have laid hands on their substance in the day of their calamity;

14. Neither shouldest thou have stood in the crossway, to cut off those of his that did escape; neither shouldest thou have delivered up those of his that did remain in the day of distress."

The Showdown

Doom against Seir

(Ezekiel **35**) "Moreover the word of the LORD came unto me, saying,

1. Son of man, set thy face against mount Seir, and prophesy against it,

2. And say unto it, Thus saith the Lord GOD; Behold, O mount Seir, I am against thee, and I will stretch out mine hand against thee, and I will make thee most desolate.

3. I will lay thy cities waste, and thou shalt be desolate, and thou shalt know that I am the LORD.

4. Because thou hast had a perpetual hatred, and hast shed the blood of the children of Israel by the force of the sword in the time of their calamity, in the time that their iniquity had an end:

5. Therefore, as I live, saith the Lord GOD, I will prepare thee unto blood, and blood shall pursue thee: sith thou hast not hated blood, even blood shall pursue thee.

6. Thus will I make mount Seir most desolate, and cut off from it him that passeth out and him that returneth.

7. And I will fill his mountains with his slain men: in thy hills, and in thy valleys, and in all thy rivers, shall they fall that are slain with the sword.

8. I will make thee perpetual desolations, and thy cities shall not return: and ye shall know that I am the LORD.

9. Because thou hast said, These two nations and these two countries shall be mine, and we will possess it; whereas the LORD was there:

10. Therefore, as I live, saith the Lord GOD, I will even do according to thine anger, and according to thine envy

which thou hast used out of thy hatred against them; and I will make myself known among them, when I have judged thee.

11. And thou shalt know that I am the LORD, and that I have heard all thy blasphemies which thou hast spoken against the mountains of Israel, saying, They are laid desolate, they are given us to consume.

12. Thus with your mouth ye have boasted against me, and have multiplied your words against me: I have heard them.

13. Thus saith the Lord God; When the whole earth rejoiceth, I will make thee   desolate.

14. As thou didst rejoice at the inheritance of the house of Israel, because it was desolate, so will I do unto thee: thou shalt be desolate, O mount Seir, and all Idumea, even all of it: and they shall know that I am the LORD."

God said They Shall Know That I Am Lord!

(Ezekiel 25) "The word of the LORD came again unto me, saying,

2. Son of man, set thy face against the Ammonites, and prophesy against them;

3. And say unto the Ammonites, Hear the word of the Lord GOD; Thus saith the Lord GOD; Because thou saidst, Aha, against my sanctuary, when it was profaned; and against the land of Israel, when it was desolate; and against the house of Judah, when they went into captivity;

4. Behold, therefore I will deliver thee to the men of the east for a possession, and they shall set their palaces in thee, and make their dwellings in thee: they shall eat thy fruit, and they shall drink thy milk.

5. And I will make Rabbah a stable for camels, and the Ammonites a couching place for flocks: and ye shall know that I am the LORD.

6. For thus saith the Lord GOD; Because thou hast clapped thine hands, and stamped with the feet, and rejoiced in heart with all thy despite against the land of Israel;

7. Behold, therefore I will stretch out mine hand upon thee, and will deliver thee for a spoil to the heathen; and I will cut thee off from the people, and I will cause thee to perish out of the countries: I will destroy thee; and thou shalt know that I am the LORD.

8. Thus saith the Lord GOD; Because that Moab and Seir do say, Behold, the house of Judah is like unto all the heathen;

9. Therefore, behold, I will open the side of Moab from the cities, from his cities which are on his frontiers, the glory of the country, Bethjeshimoth, Baalmeon, and Kiriathaim,

10. Unto the men of the east with the Ammonites, and will give them in possession, that the Ammonites may not be remembered among the nations.

11. And I will execute judgments upon Moab; and they shall know that I am the LORD.

12. Thus saith the Lord GOD; Because that Edom hath dealt against the house of Judah by taking

vengeance, and hath greatly offended, and revenged himself upon them;

13. Therefore thus saith the Lord God; I will also stretch out mine hand upon Edom, and will cut off man and beast from it; and I will make it desolate from Teman; and they of Dedan shall fall by the sword.

14. And I will lay my vengeance upon Edom by the hand of my people Israel: and they shall do in Edom according to mine anger and according to my fury; and they shall know my vengeance, saith the Lord God.

15. Thus saith the Lord God; Because the Philistines have dealt by revenge, and have taken vengeance with a despiteful heart, to destroy it for the old hatred;

16. Therefore thus saith the Lord God; Behold, I will stretch out mine hand upon the Philistines, and I will cut off the Cherethims, and destroy the remnant of the sea coast.

17. And I will execute great vengeance upon them with furious rebukes; and they shall know that I am the Lord, when I shall lay my vengeance upon them."

4 CRAFTSMEN

The Craftsman are going to strike terror into the hearts of the likes of Assyria and Babylon.

(Zechariah 1:20-21 KJV) "Then the Lord showed me four craftsmen. And I said, "What are these coming to do?**

So he said, "These *are* the horns that scattered Judah, so that no one could lift up his head; but [a]the craftsmen are coming to terrify them, to cast out the horns of the nations that lifted up *their* horn against the land of Judah to scatter it."

(Genesis 27:33 KJV) "And Isaac trembled very exceedingly, and said, Who? where is he that hath taken venison, and brought it me, and I have eaten of all before thou camest, and have blessed him? yea, and he shall be blessed."

Wake up Israel

DECEPTION… We were lied to, beaten, scattered, misused, and abused, but we are also blinded due to a lack of submission to God. Disobedience to God's laws has led us to a spiraling disconnect from God. We have placed other gods before him and worshiped them and not the Creator. The good news is that God is Love. Eager to forgive us as soon as we come to him and **_REPENT_**.

God is faithful and is just; a keeper of His word. He is full of grace and mercy, and very compassionate towards us!
The promise given to Father Abraham then to Isaac then To Jacob (Israel), **The Plan Of Salvation,** will be fulfilled for his name's sake.

(1 John 1: 9 KJV) "If we confess our sins, he is faithful and just to forgive us our sins, and to cleanse us from all unrighteousness."

(Psalm 86: 5 KJV) "For thou, Lord, *art* good, and ready to forgive; and plenteous in mercy unto all them that call upon thee."

MARCH AROUND JERICHO

Joshua led the Israelites to bring down the walls of Jericho. A powerful act that demonstrates the faithfulness and might of our Lord. The narrative is part of the fulfillment of the greater promise that God made to the Israelites that they would indeed enter the Promised Land.
(6)

SOUND THE ALARM

(Joel 2:1 KJV) "Blow ye the trumpet in Zion, and sound an alarm in my holy mountain: let all the inhabitants of the land tremble: for the day of the LORD cometh, for it is nigh at hand;"

The House of Israel Must Be Gathered. God's Mercy. God will Restore Judah & Israel.

(Jeremiah 23:3 KJV) "And I will gather the remnant of my flock out of all the countries whither I have driven them, and will bring them again to their folds; and they shall be fruitful and increase."

(Jeremiah 33: 7 KJV) "And I will cause the captivity of Judah and the captivity of Israel to return, and will build them, as at the first."

Weapons for battle Israel:

(2 Corinthians 10: 4-5 KJV) "(For the weapons of our warfare are not carnal, but mighty through God to the pulling down of strong holds;)

5 Casting down imaginations, and every high thing that exalteth

itself against the knowledge of God, and bringing into captivity

every thought to the obedience of Christ;"

Song: We are climbing Jacob's ladder children, Soldiers of the

Cross.

Who are the **144,000**? Where are they from?
Answer: From all the Tribes of the children of Israel

(Revelation 7:4 KJV) "And I heard the number of them which were
sealed: and there were sealed an hundred and forty and four
thousand of all the tribes of the children of
Israel."

Oh ye dry bones, hear the word of the Lord!
(Ezekiel 37: 4-8 KJV) "Again he said unto me, Prophesy upon
these bones, and say unto them, O ye dry bones, hear the
word of the LORD.
5.   Thus saith the Lord GOD unto these bones; Behold, I
      will cause breath to enter into you, and ye shall live:
6.   And I will lay sinews upon you, and will bring up flesh
      upon you, and cover you with skin, and put breath in
      you, and ye shall live; and ye shall know that I am the
      LORD.
7.   So I prophesied as I was commanded: and as I
      prophesied, there was a noise, and behold a shaking,
      and the bones came together, bone to his bone.

The covenant that God made with Israel has a significant role in securing the world, as it signifies the Lord's salvation. God chose Israel as His cherished possession, and out of all the nations, He made them His people. Despite their unfaithfulness and at times, open rebellion, God remains faithful to His covenant and continues to take care of His flock.
(7)

God chose the lineage of Jacob, also known as Israel, from which the Messiah, Jesus, would come. This was part of his plan of redemption to save all of mankind. Through Jesus, all people, regardless of their background, can become part of the family of God. Those who have accepted Jesus as their savior are not defined by their ethnicity, but are united as one kingdom family. They have a mission to share the gospel with the world and bring others into this chosen family of believers.

NO LONGER JEW NOR GENTILE - ONE KINGDOM

(Galatians 3: 28-29 KJV) "There is neither Jew nor Greek, there is neither bond nor free, there is neither male nor female: for ye are all one in Christ Jesus.
And if ye be Christ's, then are ye Abraham's seed, and heirs according to the promise."

Who / what does a follower of Christ or a child of God look like?

(2 Corinthians 5:17 KJV) "Therefore if any man be in Christ, he is a new creature; old things are passed away; behold, all things are become new."

(Galatians 5: 22-23 KJV) "But the fruit of the Spirit is love, joy, peace, longsuffering, gentleness, goodness, faith,

Meekness, temperance: against such there is no law."

Throughout the Bible, we see examples of individuals who were chosen by God to be Israelites. However, being an Israelite was not just a matter of birth; it was also about having faith in God. When we accept Jesus and live by his teachings, we become new creations and are united as one. It is essential to live our lives according to Jesus' word and strive to reflect his character of perfect love. God is love.

Do Not Be Embarrassed To Share Jesus!

(Matthew 10:33 KJV) "But whosoever shall deny me before men, him will I also deny before my Father which is in heaven."

There has been a lot of new information in the past few days. I have opened myself up to God's guidance to see the truth. The truth must be revealed. As followers of Christ, we must come together as one. God has promised that if we seek Him, we will find Him. However, to see events unfold, we must abide by, obey, and trust in God. We must prepare ourselves, like the five wise virgins, to meet our groom.

CHAPTER VI

THE SHOWDOWN

The Showdown

(Hebrews 10:37 KJV) "For yet a little while, and he that shall come will come, and will not tarry."

(Revelation 6: 7-8 KJV) "And when he had opened the fourth seal, I heard the voice of the fourth beast say, Come and see.

And I looked, and behold a pale horse: and his name that sat on him was Death, and Hell followed with him. And power was given unto them over the fourth part of the earth, to kill with sword, and with hunger, and with death, and with the beasts of the earth."

FAITH

(Hebrews 11:1 KJV) "Now faith is the substance of things hoped for, the evidence of things not seen."

We can only be saved by God. There is a battle happening, but it has already been won. Our creator, God, sent his only son, Jesus, to save the world through him. The only way we can make it is by having faith in Jesus. We must believe that He exists and that He rewards those who earnestly seek Him.

(Hebrews 11: 6 KJV) "But without faith *it is* impossible to please *him*: for he that cometh to God must believe that he is, and *that* he is a rewarder of them that diligently seek him."

ABIDE

(John 15:7 KJV) "If ye abide in me, and my words abide in you, ye shall ask what ye will, and it shall be done unto you."

A vital aspect of our faith is staying connected to God through Christ as we recognize that we can do nothing without Him. We should strive to maintain this connection with God daily, seeking His renewal and mercies. As we surrender to Him, God fills us with His love and power to overcome challenges. He guides us to His will and brings about positive changes in our lives and those around us. Through His love, God offers redemption and salvation to all who believe and trust in Him. When we obey and allow Him to lead our lives, we become new creations in Him. God is a loving and compassionate God who hears us and is always close to us.

(Psalm 34: 18-20 KJV) "The LORD is nigh unto them that are of a broken heart; and saveth such as be of a contrite spirit.
19 Many are the afflictions of the righteous: but the LORD delivereth him out of them all.**20** He keepeth all his bones: not one of them is broken."

STAND

(Revelation 6:17 KJV) "For the great day of his wrath is come; and who shall be able to stand?"

As we approach the soon return of Christ, we are reminded that we have been called for such a time as this. It is our duty to stand firm and put on the whole armor of God. We need to build a strong relationship with Him based on His Holy word. We should prepare our homes, minds, and hearts as we share the gospel and eagerly await His arrival. Let us fight the good fight of faith, knowing that we will be renewed and strengthened.

(1 Timothy 6:12 KJV) "Fight the good fight of faith, lay hold on eternal life, whereunto thou art also called, and hast professed a good profession before many witnesses."

(Isaiah 40:31 KJV) "But they that wait upon the LORD shall renew their strength; they shall mount up with wings as eagles; they shall run, and not be weary; and they shall walk, and not faint."

(Ephesians 6: 13-18 KJV) "Wherefore take unto you the whole armour of God, that ye may be able to withstand in the evil day, and having done all, to stand.

> Stand therefore, having your loins girt about with truth, and having on the breastplate of righteousness;
> And your feet shod with the preparation of the gospel of peace;
> Above all, taking the shield of faith, wherewith ye shall be able to quench all the fiery darts of the wicked.
> And take the helmet of salvation, and the sword of the Spirit, which is the word of God:
> Praying always with all prayer and supplication in the Spirit, and watching thereunto with all perseverance and supplication for all saints;"

Do Not Worry. God Always Provides!

(Matthew 6:26 KJV) " Behold the fowls of the air: for they sow not, neither do they reap, nor gather into barns; yet your heavenly Father feedeth them. Are ye not much better than they?"

We serve a God who keeps His covenant with His children. Before we even knew Him, we were called and chosen. We are wonderfully and fearfully made by a Creator who promised to never leave us nor forsake us. He is our refuge and promises to protect us. We are a unique and special people, made in the image of God. He reminds us not to worry, for He is our shepherd who will provide for all of our needs. He will comfort us, be with us, and give us everything we need.

(Psalm 139: 14 KJV) "I will praise thee; for I am fearfully and wonderfully made: Marvelous are thy works; And that my soul knoweth right well."

The Showdown

(Psalm 91 KJV) "He that dwelleth in the secret place of the most High shall abide under the shadow of the Almighty.

2.   I will say of the LORD, He is my refuge and my fortress: my God; in him will I trust.

3.   Surely he shall deliver thee from the snare of the fowler, and from the noisome pestilence.

4.   He shall cover thee with his feathers, and under his wings shalt thou trust: his truth shall be thy shield and buckler.

5.   Thou shalt not be afraid for the terror by night; nor for the arrow that flieth by day;

6.   Nor for the pestilence that walketh in darkness; nor for the destruction that wasteth at noonday.

7.   A thousand shall fall at thy side, and ten thousand at thy right hand; but it shall not come nigh thee.

8.   Only with thine eyes shalt thou behold and see the reward of the wicked.

9.   Because thou hast made the LORD, which is my refuge, even the most High, thy habitation;

10.   There shall no evil befall thee, neither shall any plague come nigh thy dwelling.

11.   For he shall give his angels charge over thee, to keep thee in all thy ways.

12.   They shall bear thee up in their hands, lest thou dash thy foot against a stone.

13.   Thou shalt tread upon the lion and adder: the young lion and the dragon shalt thou trample under feet.

14.   Because he hath set his love upon me, therefore will I deliver him: I will set him on high, because he hath known my name.

15.   He shall call upon me, and I will answer him: I will be with him in trouble; I will deliver him, and honour him.

16.   With long life will I satisfy him, and shew him my salvation."

The Showdown

(Isaiah 43: 2 KJV) "When thou passest through the waters, I will be with thee; and through the rivers, they shall not overflow thee: when thou walkest through the fire, thou shalt not be burned; neither shall the flame kindle upon thee."

(Hebrews 13: 5 KJV)
 "Let your conversation *be* without covetousness; *and be* content with such things as ye have: for he hath said, I will never leave thee, nor for sake thee."

The Great Controversy

The final showdown is imminent. He who is expected will arrive soon without any delay. The devil and his kingdom, which have been causing chaos and destruction, will finally be defeated. Despite making his final attempts to throw his wicked darts at the followers of Christ, he will eventually be overthrown.
The devil has been deceiving God's people for centuries. His ultimate goal has always been to distract us from God and steer us away from the path of righteousness. He is always seeking to kill, steal, and destroy. However, his time is up, and his reign is coming to an end. In the end, God triumphs over evil. The battle is already won!

(2 Thessalonians 2: 9 KJV) "Even him, whose coming is after the working of Satan with all power and signs and lying wonders,"

(Revelation 12:12 KJV) "Therefore rejoice, ye heavens, and ye that dwell in them. Woe to the inhabiters of the earth and of the sea! for the devil is come down unto you, having great wrath, because he knoweth that he hath but a short time."

The Showdown

The antichrist

(Revelation 13:15 KJV) "And he had power to give life unto the image of the beast, that the image of the beast should both speak, and cause that as many as would not worship the image of the beast should be killed."

The Beast has already been revived and it's just a matter of time before the antichrist will be revealed to the world.

Who is the antichrist?
Answer: The one who signs the Israeli's war peace treaty, is the antichrist.

(2 Thessalonians 2: 4 KJV) "Who opposeth and exalteth himself above all that is called God, or that is worshipped; so that he as God sitteth in the temple of God, shewing himself that he is God."

Wage war against the people of God; Those who keep the testimonies of Jesus.

Revelation (12:17 KJV) "And the dragon was wroth with the woman, and went to make war with the remnant of her seed, which keep the commandments of God, and have the testimony of Jesus Christ."

Revelation 13: 7 KJV) "And it was given unto him to make war with the saints, and to overcome them: and power was given him over all kindreds; and tongues; and nations."

A one-world government will be established, and the world will be astonished. This will lead to a time of persecution for those who hold fast to the testimonies of God and the faith of Jesus. Be prepared!

(Revelation 13: 3 KJV) "And I saw one of his heads as it were wounded to death; and his deadly wound was healed: and all the world wondered after the beast."

(Revelation 13:16-17 KJV) "And he causeth all, both small and great, rich and poor, free and bond, to receive a mark in their right hand, or in their foreheads:
And that no man might buy or sell, save he that had the mark, or the name of the beast, or the number of his name.

The Abomination Desolation

The devil wants to be worshipped. There is a battle being waged against the Lord's Day, and Satan will make his final attempts to change the Lord's 7th day Sabbath to Sunday. This change will be enforced and mandated by law. The 7th day Sabbath serves as a testimony that we worship the God of Abraham, Isaac, and Jacob and that He is the Creator who formed the earth in six days and rested on the Sabbath day.

The 4TH COMMANDMENT - THE SABBATH

(Exodus 20: 8 KJV) "Remember the sabbath day, to keep it holy."

WHEN IS THE SABBATH?

(Exodus 20:10 KJV) "But the seventh day is the sabbath of the Lord thy God."

The Sabbath Day - The 7th Day

(Exodus 20: 11 KJV) "For in six days the Lord made heaven and earth, the sea, and all that in them is, and rested the seventh day:"

Who is the SABBATH, for?

(Mark 2: 27-28 KJV) "And he said unto them, The sabbath was made for man, and not man for the sabbath:
Therefore the Son of man is Lord also of the Sabbath."

?? So who changed Sabbath to Sunday?
Answer: On March 7, 321, Roman Emperor Constantine I declared Sunday a day of rest for judges, city people, and craftsmen, stating that they should rest on the venerable day of the sun.
(8)

Which pope changed the Sabbath to Sunday?
Pope Sylvester

In 325 A.D., Pope Sylvester declared Sunday as "the Lord's Day." Later, in 338 A.D., Eusebius, the bishop of Constantine's court, wrote that all the tasks that were originally meant to be done on the Sabbath (the seventh day of the week) were now to be done on the Lord's Day (the first day of the week).
(9)

?? Does anyone / any man have the right to change the Lord's day?
Answer: NO

(Deuteronomy 4: 2 KJV) "Ye shall not add unto the word which I command you, neither shall ye diminish ought from it, that ye may keep the commandments of the Lord your God which I command you."

(Revelation 22: 18-19 KJV) "For I testify unto every man that heareth the words of the prophecy of this book, If any man shall add unto these things, God shall add unto him the plagues that are written in this book:
¹⁹ And if any man shall take away from the words of the book of this prophecy, God shall take away his part out of the book of life, and out of the holy city, and from the things which are written in this book."

When you see The Abomination of Desolation, Run!

(Matthew 24: 15-22 KJV) "When ye therefore shall see the abomination of desolation, spoken of by Daniel the prophet, stand in the holy place, (whoso readeth, let him understand:)

9. Then let them which be in Judaea flee into the mountains:
10. Let him which is on the housetop not come down to take any thing out of his house:
11. Neither let him which is in the field return back to take his clothes.
12. And woe unto them that are with child, and to them that give suck in those days!
13. But pray ye that your flight be not in the winter, neither on the sabbath day:
14. For then shall be great tribulation, such as was not since the beginning of the world to this time, no, nor ever shall be.
15. And except those days should be shortened, there should no flesh be saved: but for the elect's sake those days shall be shortened."

(Mark 13:14 KJV) "But when ye shall see the abomination of desolation, spoken of by Daniel the prophet, standing where it ought not, (let him that readeth understand,) then let them that be in Judaea flee to the mountains:"

There is a time of unprecedented trouble ahead. This confirms our place in God's kingdom and His mission of salvation for humankind.

(Matthew 24: 37-39 KJV) " But as the days of Noah were, so shall also the coming of the Son of man be.

38.   For as in the days that were before the flood they were eating and drinking, marrying and giving in marriage, until the day that Noe entered into the ark,

39.   And knew not until the flood came, and took them all away; so shall also the coming of the Son of man be."

The Great Tribulation (later 3 ½ of tribulation), starts when the antichrist is revealed in the third temple.

(Daniel 9:27 KJV) "And he shall confirm the covenant with many for one week: and in the midst of the week he shall cause the sacrifice and the oblation to cease, and for the overspreading of abominations he shall make it desolate, even until the consummation, and that determined shall be poured upon the desolate."

ARMAGEDDON:

In the ultimate confrontation between good and evil, Satan will use every trick in his arsenal to mislead and annihilate the remaining faithful followers of God. Although he knows that his time is running out, he is fully aware that the victory ultimately belongs to God.

(Revelation 16:14 KJV) "For they are the spirits of devils, working miracles, which go forth unto the kings of the earth and of the whole world, to gather them to the battle of that great day of God Almighty."

(Revelation 16:16 KJV) "And he gathered them together into a place called in the Hebrew tongue Armageddon."

God's Mission, Our Mission!

We have been commissioned to spread the gospel of Christ to the world. God, our creator, gave us his only begotten son, Jesus, who came and died on the cross for all our sins. We must worship Him as it is He who created the heavens, the earth, the sea, and the fountains of water.

Time is running out, and it is more urgent than ever to share the three angels' message. As long as I am alive, I will share the love of Jesus and what He has done for me. We must remove ourselves from Babylon's false worship and idols which cannot save us. Our faith in Christ Jesus alone can save us by His grace, for it was the price that Jesus paid when His blood was shed on Calvary's cross for us all.

3 ANGELS MESSAGE

1. **Fear God, he is the creator, He made you.**
2. **Get out of Babylon, stop idol/false worship**
3. **DO NOT RECEIVE THE MARK OF THE BEAST - STAY CLEAR**

(Revelation 14: 6-11 KJV) "And I saw another angel fly in the midst of heaven, having the everlasting gospel to preach unto them that dwell on the earth, and to every nation, and kindred, and tongue, and people,

7. Saying with a loud voice, Fear God, and give glory to him; for the hour of his judgment is come: and worship him that made heaven, and earth, and the sea, and the fountains of waters.

8. And there followed another angel, saying, Babylon is fallen, is fallen, that great city, because she made all nations drink of the wine of the wrath of her fornication.

9. And the third angel followed them, saying with a loud voice, If any man worship the beast and his image, and receive his mark in his forehead, or in his hand, [1]

10. The same shall drink of the wine of the wrath of God, which is poured out without mixture into the cup of his indignation; and he shall be tormented with fire and brimstone in the presence of the holy angels, and in the presence of the Lamb:

11. And the smoke of their torment ascendeth up for ever and ever: and they have no rest day nor night, who worship the beast and his image, and whosoever receiveth the mark of his name."

Jesus Is The Answer!

As the time for our redemption draws near, we must remember that only Jesus can save us. Every day, as humans, we should pray, praise, and celebrate the fact that God sent us His most valuable gift - Jesus. We must be grateful because the wages of sin is death, and that is where we were headed. Due to our stubborn, disobedient, stiff-necked, and idolatrous ways, Jesus came to be the propitiation for our sins.

The Showdown

Jesus is the Way the Truth and the Life! There is no other way to the Father but by Him.

(John 14: 6 KJV) "Jesus saith unto him, I am the way, the truth, and the life: no man cometh unto the Father, but by me."

(1 John 2:2 KJV) "And he is the propitiation for our sins: and not for ours only, but also for the sins of the whole world."

The Gospel to the World - One Kingdom of God

Great and encouraging news for all nations, kindreds, tongues, and peoples. We don't have to perish anymore but can have eternal, everlasting life with our Lord and Savior, Jesus Christ. God is willing to forgive us of our sins if we REPENT. He is a Father who listens to our cries and carries our deepest sorrows. He is a God who says, "Come unto me and I will give you rest." He is a shepherd to one fold and the God of hope who keeps His promises. You can stand with Him because He is a covenant keeper!

(John 3:16 KJV) "For God so loved the world, that he gave his only begotten Son, that whosoever believeth in him should not perish, but have everlasting life."

(John 10:16 KJV) "And other sheep I have, which are not of this fold: them also I must bring, and they shall hear my voice; and there shall be one fold, and one shepherd."

(Matthew 11: 28-29 KJV) "Come unto me, all ye that labour and are heavy laden, and I will give you rest.
29 Take my yoke upon you, and learn of me; for I am meek and lowly in heart: and ye shall find rest unto your souls."

AN ARMY

An army of God is rising up and preparing for a ready mission. The harvest is plentiful, and many people are waiting to hear about Jesus. So, onward forward, ye soldiers of the cross! Pray, prepare, and be ready, with your feet shod with the everlasting gospel of peace. The kingdom of God is at hand, and He is calling all of His children - whether Greek, Jew, or Gentile - all who are willing to choose Him and want to be saved.

(Matthew 9: 37-38 KJV) "Then saith he unto his disciples, The harvest truly is plenteous, but the labourers are few;
38 Pray ye therefore the Lord of the harvest, that he will send forth labourers into his harvest."

(Ephesians 6:15 KJV) "And your feet shod with the preparation of the gospel of peace;"

(Matthew 28: 19-20 KJV) "Go ye therefore, and teach all nations, baptizing them in the name of the Father, and of the Son, and of the Holy Ghost:
Teaching them to observe all things whatsoever I have commanded you: and lo, I am with you always, even unto the end of the world."

Bibliography

1. The Holy Bible - King
    James Version

2. Image 2nd temple pg 20
The Smithsonian magazine @ smithsonianmag.com

3. Third temple pg 21
https://www.smithsonianmag.com/history/what-is-beneath-the-temple-mount-920764/#:~:text=Today%20the%20Tem ple%20Mount%2C%20a,the%20holiest%20site%20in%20Judaism. The Abomination of Desolation
https://www.onethingministries.net/wp/wp-content/IHOP-OTM-ET-Introductory-Series—-Session-12.pdf

4. Lineage photo pg 26 -
    biblestudy.org

5. The Promised Land - Pg
    27
    https://bibleproject.com/articles/land-thermometer-covenantal-faithfulness/

6. March around Jericho
    pg 38
    https://www.biblestudytools.com/bible-study/topical-studies/powerful-lessons-from-th e-fall-of-the-walls-of-jericho.html

7. God's covenant special role pg 40 pg 20 Adult Sabbath School Bible Study Guide - Jan/Feb/Mar2024 - Psalms- published by Pacific Press ISSN 1096-7400)

8. Who changed Sabbath to Sunday? Pg 47 Sabbath in Christianity - Wikipedia W

9. Which pope changed Sabbath to Sunday? Pg 47

https://www.sabbathtruth.com › story Where's the Evidence That the Sabbath Was Changed?)

Made in the USA
Columbia, SC
22 June 2024

37320279R00048